NATIONAL GEOGRAPHIC

Ladders

NATIVE AMERICANS OF THE GREAT PLAINS

HORSE

The Lakota people live in the Great Plains. This photo was taken around 1905. It shows two men on horseback wearing feather headdresses. Only the powerful Lakota men wore these headdresses. They earned each feather through special deeds.

by Joseph Markham

If you're like most Americans, a car is part of your life. It gets you where you need to go. It helps your family get food, supplies, and other things you need. Do you ever think about what life was like before cars?

Early Native Americans of the Great Plains didn't have cars, but they had something equally helpful—the horse. When we think of Native Americans, especially on the plains, we often picture them on horseback. But did you know that the horse was not always a part of life on the Great Plains?

The descendants of the horses brought to North America by the Spanish are called mustangs. This wild herd of mustangs is charging through the deserts of Utah.

POWER

When the first Native Americans came to the Great Plains, there were no horses. Before the horse, Native Americans traveled everywhere on foot or by boat. It took a long time to get from place to place, so they didn't travel very long distances.

When the Spanish arrived in the Americas during the 1500s, they brought horses with them. This changed life for Native Americans on the Great Plains in nearly every way. On the next few pages, we'll look at just a few of the ways horses changed life for the people on the plains.

Before the Horse

People have always settled near rivers, lakes, and other waterways to have water for drinking and washing. Water is also useful for getting from one place to another. Early Native Americans traveled on waterways, moving swiftly in canoes carved from tree trunks. When they had to pass over land between rivers or lakes, they would carry their canoes above their heads.

Before the horse, Native Americans couldn't always count on trading to get the things they needed. Because of the time it took to travel on foot to trading posts, where they bought, sold, and traded goods, people often just shared belongings with the rest of their tribe.

Long travel times also kept people closer to home. Before the horse, most Plains people lived in settled villages. They built homes of dirt and grass that were partially underground to keep them cool in summer and warm in winter.

When they did need to travel longer distances, Native Americans used dogs to help them move their belongings. Dogs were more than pets to Native Americans—they were helpers. The tribes carried their belongings on a travois (truh-VOY), a kind of sled that a dog could pull.

Many Plains Native Americans lived in houses made of dirt and grass when they weren't traveling.

A travois (shown at center below) is a wooden frame that looks like a long triangle. This illustration shows two dogs pulling travois across the plains.

After the Horse

After horses were brought to the area, the Native Americans' way of life changed forever. On horseback, they could travel farther and move faster than ever before while carrying much heavier loads. With the horse, many tribes of the plains became **nomadic**. They would move from place to place, following thundering herds of buffalo. In late spring and summer, the buffalo would stop to gather in big groups to give birth and to take care of the baby buffalo. At this time, the tribes would stop traveling to hunt the buffalo herds.

Many Great Plains tribes also began to live in more temporary structures that fit their nomadic lifestyle. The **tipi**, a tent made of animal skins, was a useful alternative to a permanent hut. The tipi was easy to put up and take down when moving to or from another place. It was the perfect choice for a Great Plains "mobile home."

Horses allowed Native Americans to travel more. With horses, larger trade networks opened up among tribes. The animals were also a valuable trading item. Because of this, they were a symbol of status. The more horses a tribe had, the more wealthy and powerful the tribe was.

Women were often in charge of setting up the tipis. They created a cone shape with thin wooden poles. Then they wrapped large animal skins around the outside of the cone.

A Native American child rides on a travois. The child sits on a platform resting between two poles that are attached to her mother's horse.

5

HUNTING
Before the Horse

The buffalo was always a big part of life on the Great Plains. Before people had horses, hunting buffalo was especially dangerous. Buffalo roamed the plains in herds, and they could **stampede** for the slightest reason, wiping out everything in their path. Plains hunters were good at outsmarting the buffalo herds, and they used many different hunting techniques.

Buffalo do not have great eyesight, and Native Americans used this against them. They disguised themselves by draping a buffalo hide or other animal skin over their bodies. Then they would creep up near the buffalo with spears in hand and attack. Or the hunters would surprise the buffalo, running after them to make them stampede toward a cliff. When the buffalo reached the cliff's edge, they could not stop, so they fell. The hunters then collected the buffalo and used them to make clothing, tipis, and other things. These hunting techniques were effective, but they also put the hunters in danger.

This painting depicts how some hunters might have hunted buffalo. They wore wolf skins as a disguise. Then they could sneak close enough to the animal to attack it.

HUNTING
After the Horse

Once the horse arrived, hunting buffalo would never be the same. While the Great Plains hunters still used many of the same tricks, with the horse they gained speed and strength. Horses could run as fast as the buffalo. On horseback, the hunters had more protection from the buffalo. They could make a quick escape if needed. Also, with horses, Native Americans could cover a wide area and carry food and water for longer hunts.

The buffalo soon became the focus of Native American life on the Great Plains and the most important source of wealth. Horses made hunting buffalo easier, and soon, tribes had many hides to trade for other goods. However, hunting buffalo and trading buffalo hides on horseback came with new risks. Sometimes tribes followed buffalo onto the land of rival tribes, or they passed through it on their way to trade. If they trespassed, or entered land that belonged to another tribe, conflicts could break out.

Hunters used their horses to force the buffalo toward their camp. More hunters waited there to attack the buffalo.

On horseback, Native Americans could make a quick getaway if the buffalo turned and stampeded.

Before the Horse

ALLIES AND ENEMIES

Tribes have had both **allies** and enemies among other tribes throughout history. Before the horse, tribes would form friendships with others living nearby, sharing resources and information. Sometimes tribes in the same area would fight over the same limited resources. If one group trespassed or stole from another, fighting would break out.

The way warriors fought before the horse was mostly through hand-to-hand combat. Small fights broke out occasionally, and ongoing conflicts might last for days, weeks, or longer. Both sides suffered heavy losses as battles dragged on.

This Native American drawing from 1833 shows a Mandan chief and a Cheyenne chief in hand-to-hand combat. Their tribes were bitter enemies.

After the Horse

The horse changed the way tribes interacted and went to war. On horseback, Native Americans were able to make contact with other tribes who lived far away. They formed relationships—and fought wars—across much bigger distances and with more tribes. New friendships formed when tribes met other groups who lived far away. In battle, friendly tribes could travel farther on horseback to help their allies. Because horses made it so easy to get around, having them gave a tribe power. Since horses were so valuable, sometimes tribes stole them from enemy tribes to weaken them.

Horses allowed Native Americans to meet new allies and trade with them. For example, they could ride to settlements where Europeans paid good money for buffalo hides and sold guns and other weapons to the Native Americans. The weapons made tribes more effective on the battlefield and on hunting grounds. These relationships and trade agreements came to be because of the freedom of movement that horses brought to the Plains people.

Men of the Crow tribe and other Native Americans trade goods.

Horses did many of the same tasks that dogs did. Some Native Americans called horses "big dogs." There was no word for *horse* in their languages.

Check In How did horses change the way the Native Americans of the Great Plains lived?

How the Horse Came to Be

retold by Sherri Patoka   illustrated by Amanda Hall

Native American stories such as this one often include a **vision quest**. During a vision quest, a person seeks advice or help from a guardian spirit. This story tells about a boy who goes searching for answers and gets help from a spirit, but it also shows the importance of horses to the Native Americans of the Great Plains.

The Blackfoot were among the earliest Native American nations to move westward and settle on the Great Plains. They became skilled buffalo hunters. When the Blackfoot people got their own horses, it made a huge difference in their lives. Read the Blackfoot folk tale—a story from the past that is known to many—about how the horse first came to them.

Many years ago, an orphan boy named Long Arrow lived among the Blackfoot because his parents had died. He felt out of place because he was not Blackfoot. He was from the Chippewa tribe. Life had not been easy for Long Arrow, but he was always looking for ways to make it better. He decided to search far and wide for the secret to happiness and strength. Long Arrow left the Blackfoot village and went off on a quest. He prayed, but his prayers went unanswered. Then he fasted, going without food for days, hoping his hunger would give him a vision of what he needed to do. Still, he found no answer, so he walked and walked through the plains, looking for a sign.

The rolling plains seemed endless to Long Arrow. In his frustration, he failed to see the beauty of the land—the flowers, the grasses, the green hills, and the winding rivers. Hopeless, exhausted, and not knowing what else to do, he knelt down beside a lake and wept.

Unknown to Long Arrow, a very old and very powerful Water Spirit dwelled beneath the surface of the lake, below where Long Arrow wept. The Water Spirit heard the young boy's weeping and felt sad for him, so he sent his own son to fetch the boy. "Go now, my son," he declared, "and bring the boy who weeps beside the lake to me." So the son of the Water Spirit swam up to the surface of the lake and greeted the weeping boy.

"Who are you, and what do you want?" the startled Long Arrow asked.

"Hurry. Come with me," the Water Spirit's son replied. "I will take you to see my father, the Water Spirit, but you must be sure to hold on tightly to my shoulders, and keep your eyes shut. Do not open them until I tell you to."

Long Arrow clutched the other boy's shoulders and closed his eyes, and the son of the Water Spirit dove deep into the lake. As they swam down through the water, the boy whispered some advice to Long Arrow: "My father will ask you which animal from the lake you would like. Choose the old mallard duck and her little ducklings." Long Arrow was puzzled by this advice, but he nodded in agreement.

Just then, Long Arrow and his guide arrived at the underwater lodge of the great Water Spirit. "You may open your eyes now," the son said. When Long Arrow did so, he saw a very old man with long white hair.

"Why are you crying, my boy?" asked the Water Spirit.

"I have had nothing but bad luck," answered Long Arrow. "I have come on a quest to find special powers that will help me make my way in the world."

"I will happily assist you in your search," said the Water Spirit. "The animals that live in this lake are mine to give. Which animal would you like?"

Without hesitation, Long Arrow replied, "The old mallard duck and her ducklings."

"That duck is so old! Why don't you choose another animal?" the Water Spirit asked.

The Water Spirit tried four times to persuade Long Arrow to change his mind, but Long Arrow's answer was always the same: "I will take the old mallard duck and her ducklings."

Finally, the Water Spirit smiled broadly and said, "My son will take you to the edge of the lake, and after dark he will catch the mallard for you. Then take the mallard and her ducklings and walk away, but do not look back."

On the bank of the lake, the Water Spirit's son caught the mallard, tied a piece of braided marsh grass around her neck like a leash, placed the end in Long Arrow's hand, and said, "You must not look back until dawn." Then Long Arrow walked away into the darkness, leading the old mallard and her ducklings, listening to the sounds of their wings flapping behind him.

Long Arrow walked all night. There came a time when he no longer heard the ducks quacking or their wings flapping, but he did not look back. Then he began to hear a heavy "clomp-clomp" behind him, but he still did not look back. Next, the braided marsh grass turned into a thick rope in his hands, but the boy still did not look back.

Finally, when the sun began to rise, Long Arrow turned around. There, on the other end of the rope, was not a duck but a magnificent horse! He mounted the horse's back and rode it to the Blackfoot camp. By the time he reached camp, he heard many more horses galloping behind him.

At first his people were surprised and frightened by the strange beasts. They called the horses "elk-dogs" because they were so big. Long Arrow gave each Blackfoot a horse, yet there were still many left to roam the plains.

They all learned how to ride, and how to use the horses to pull and carry their belongings. It was much easier to cross rivers on horses. It was also easier to find buffalo herds and to hunt the buffalo. The people were delighted with the horses and with Long Arrow.

When he grew older, the Blackfoot made Long Arrow a chief because of the wonderful gift he had brought to them. The orphan boy's luck had finally changed!

Check In   What rule did Long Arrow have to follow once he accepted the Water Spirit's gift?

17

Crazy Horse

by Jennifer A. Smith

A Black Hills Warrior

They say that some are born to greatness. Stories about Lakota chief Crazy Horse's bravery began when he was still a boy. By the time he was 12 years old, it is said that he had already killed his first buffalo. When he was 16, he saved his friend, a famous warrior, in a battle with another tribe. Avoiding a stream of flying arrows, Crazy Horse helped his friend onto his own horse. Together they rode away to safety. As a young man, he showed signs of being a great warrior and leader.

Crazy Horse was born around 1842 in the Black Hills of what is now South Dakota. The Black Hills were, and still are, **sacred** land to the Lakota tribe, which means that the area is deeply respected. Crazy Horse grew up with a deep sense of how important this land was to his family and his people. It was the land on which his ancestors had lived, fought, and died. His courage seemed to come from this love of his homeland. Of course he would fight to defend it.

< The Black Hills are located in South Dakota and Wyoming. They are a small mountain range that rise out of the western Great Plains.

Battle of the Little Bighorn

As more settlers traveled west across North America, they claimed the land to farm and the mountains to mine for metals and precious stones. But Native Americans already occupied much of the land out west. Conflicts started to break out between some Native Americans and settlers. **Treaties**, or formal agreements, with the U.S. government settled some conflicts between settlers and Native Americans. But too often, the treaties were ignored and conflicts would start all over again.

In 1874, Lieutenant Colonel George A. Custer led U.S. Army soldiers into Crazy Horse's territory on a successful search for gold. Drawn by the possibility of making their fortunes on gold-rich land, people flooded into the area during what is known as a **gold rush**. As more settlers arrived, tensions with Native Americans increased. Two years later, the government ordered

Artist William Herbert Dunton created this painting. He wanted to show how he imagined the action at the Battle of the Little Bighorn.

the Native Americans in the area to move onto **reservations** and give up their land to the fortune-seeking settlers.

Some groups agreed, but others joined together to resist the move. Crazy Horse, Sitting Bull, Little Big Man, and other local chiefs refused to move. Crazy Horse organized 1,200 warriors to stop the soldiers who came to move them off their land. It worked! A week later, a force of about 1,500 Native Americans—mostly Lakota and Cheyenne—defeated about 650 soldiers led by Custer. More than 200 U.S. soldiers died in the fierce battle, including Custer and all the troops immediately under his command.

The fight is known as the Battle of the Little Bighorn, named after a river nearby. It is also known as "Custer's Last Stand."

Custer was determined to fight the Native Americans, but he had underestimated their numbers and their power. Because of this foolishness, Custer and all of his men died in the battle. A short time later, the U.S. government forced Crazy Horse to surrender. He died in a struggle with soldiers a little more than a year after his great victory at the Battle of the Little Bighorn.

Lieutenant Colonel George A. Custer made serious mistakes during the Battle of the Little Bighorn. He underestimated the Native Americans' power.

My lands are where my dead lie buried.
—CHIEF CRAZY HORSE

∧ This huge sculpture of Crazy Horse's face was carved with chisels and dynamite. It is part of a larger, unfinished sculpture shown below at right.

< This model shows visitors how the sculpture at right will look when it is finished.

Crazy Horse's Legacy

Crazy Horse is remembered as one of the greatest Native American leaders of all time. He fought to preserve the Black Hills for his people, the Lakota, but unfortunately, they were not allowed to keep most of their original lands. Today, the Lakota still live in the Black Hills, but they live on reservations that cover only a small part of the sacred lands they once called home.

In 1980, the U.S. Supreme Court ruled that the U.S. government had taken the Lakota's land illegally. The Court awarded the Lakota money in payment for the land, but the Lakota refused it. They wanted their traditional lands back, not the money. If they agreed to take the money, it would mean that they agreed to sell the land. They vowed never to give up the fight, and many Lakota who continue to live on reservations in the area are still fighting for their original lands today. Crazy Horse's spirit lives on in the Lakota people's dedication to their land.

To celebrate Crazy Horse's legacy, an artist and a Lakota chief raised money to carve the Crazy Horse Memorial, a huge sculpture of Crazy Horse, on a rocky mountain in the Black Hills. Once it is completed, the memorial will be the largest mountain carving in the world.

LAKOTA MEDICINE MAN BLACK ELK'S MEMORY OF CRAZY HORSE

"People would find [Crazy Horse] out alone in the cold, and they would ask him to come home with them. He would not come, but sometimes he would tell the people what to do. People wondered if he ate anything at all. Once my father found him out alone like that, and he said to my father: 'Uncle, you have noticed me, the way I act. But do not worry; there are caves and holes for me to live in, and out here the spirits may help me. I am making plans for the good of my people.'"

Check In Why did the U.S. government force Crazy Horse and his people to move onto reservations?

Read to find out why buffalo are important to Native Americans of the Great Plains.

THE Mighty Buffalo

by Jennifer A. Smith

∧ The buffalo is the heaviest land mammal in North America.

A Hairy Situation

If you come across a buffalo at a national park, be careful! A bull, or male buffalo, is taller than the average man and weighs about 1,800 pounds. With his bad eyesight, he might not see you at first, but that might not be a good thing. You really don't want to startle a buffalo.

After his size, the second thing you might notice about the buffalo, also known as a bison, is the thick hair of his mane and beard. Touching a buffalo is not recommended, but if you did, you would feel both long, coarse hair and shorter, woolly hair. A buffalo has two different lengths of hair to keep him cool in the summer and warm in the winter. His hair is so good at protecting him in winter that snow sticks to it and doesn't melt onto his skin, making him cold. The buffalo simply has to shake the snow off of his body.

A buffalo's sharp horns and hooves look dangerous. His rolling eyes and the hot air huffing from his nostrils can be pretty scary, too. Watching buffalo from a distance is your best bet. But they are really only dangerous if they are threatened. If you watch buffalo graze on grass along the rivers of the Great Plains or cool off in a mud bath, you can see that they are gentle giants.

At one time, many millions of buffalo roamed throughout the American West. There were so many that the sounds their hooves made trampling across the plains earned them the nickname "thunder of the plains." In the mid-1800s, many hunters came west on newly completed railroads. They came to stalk the huge, fast animals for the challenge and sport of it. Sometimes they even shot them from inside the train cars they rode in. Settlers also killed buffalo for food, and traders sold buffalo meat and hides. As a result, millions of these magnificent animals were killed, and eventually, only a few hundred buffalo were left. They came close to **extinction**.

Remembering the Buffalo

The loss of the buffalo was devastating to all of the Plains tribes. They relied on the animal for everything—clothing, food, even shelter. Because of its importance, the buffalo came to symbolize both comfort and abundance. It provided soft, warm clothing, as well as food for Plains peoples. Tribes even performed **rituals**, or sacred ceremonies, centered around the buffalo.

For example, Plains people often performed a Buffalo Dance at the beginning of the hunting season in hopes of helping the hunters find the herds. In this dance, performers would paint themselves and dress up in buffalo hides. Dancers moved like buffalo to honor them. This dance was an important ritual and a gesture of respect for the animal.

Even though American settlers were overhunting the buffalo, the U.S. government did not try to stop them. Native Americans could be forced onto reservations more easily if there were no more buffalo to hunt. Without buffalo, there would be no hides to trade. Plains tribes often traded buffalo hides for goods they needed, such as guns. Guns made buffalo hunting easier and gave tribes a way to defend themselves. But even worse than no hides, without buffalo, there was no food. Desperate Native Americans would move to reservations just to survive.

The last buffalo hunt for many Plains tribes took place in 1883. After that, there were not enough buffalo left to hunt.

Buffalo robes kept people warm during the icy winters on the plains.

Native Americans of the Great Plains made shoes out of animal hides. This pair is made of buffalo.

Plains Indians often recorded important events by painting buffalo hides. This painted hide depicts a dance after a successful hunt.

Buffalo Bill's Wild West Shows

William F. Cody was responsible for introducing the buffalo to Americans living outside of the Great Plains. He got his nickname "Buffalo Bill" by winning a buffalo-hunting competition. In a single two-year period, Cody was personally responsible for killing more than 4,200 buffalo. At that time, Cody worked for a railroad company. Cody's team was laying metal railroad tracks across the plains, and his job was to provide his fellow railroad workers with meals. Hunting buffalo was the easiest way to feed all of those men.

In 1883, Buffalo Bill put on his first Wild West show. His shows featured actors revealing to the audience what life was like in the Wild West. They included cowboys, Native Americans, and many other characters who lived in the West. Buffalo Bill's company toured the United States and Europe for 30 years. Audiences were thrilled by the sight of buffalo stomping around the fairgrounds as performers acted out the hunt. Even though Buffalo Bill had made his name by killing buffalo, it was his Wild West shows that made Americans aware of how close the buffalo really was to extinction.

Native Americans were an important part of Buffalo Bill's Wild West show. However, they had to reenact and lose a battle with "U.S. Army" soldiers each night.

Buffalo Bill's Wild West show provided a family-friendly glimpse into life in the American West. It was a popular show in the United States and Europe.

Before starting his own Wild West shows, Buffalo Bill Cody took part in a staged buffalo hunt for tourists at Niagara Falls.

Custer State Park is in the Black Hills of South Dakota. The buffalo here are protected and carefully looked after to keep them healthy.

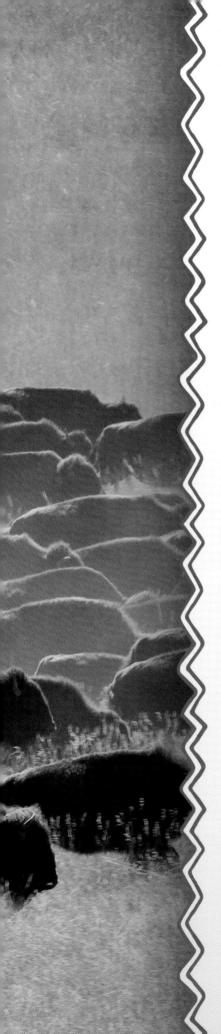

Return of the Buffalo

Thanks to **conservationists**, the buffalo has made a comeback. Starting around 1900, concerned people started working to conserve, or protect, the nation's natural resources, including the buffalo. They persuaded cattle ranchers to start raising herds of buffalo to ensure the animal wouldn't die out. Ranchers raised buffalo to sell for meat and to sell to other ranchers. Some of the ranchers' buffalo were sent to live on protected land.

In 1908, a piece of land in Montana was set aside for buffalo to graze on without being hunted. This land is called a **refuge**. The National Bison Range is one of the oldest wildlife refuges in the United States. It supports up to 500 buffalo.

Another successful buffalo conservation project was started in Yellowstone National Park. As the first national park, Yellowstone is the only place in the country where buffalo have roamed nonstop since prehistoric times. It has the largest population of buffalo living on public land—about 3,000 buffalo. Signs throughout the park warn visitors to keep at least 25 yards away from the buffalo. Remember their large size and sharp horns—buffalo can be dangerous.

The buffalo population will never return to the millions that once roamed the Great Plains, but the efforts of the government, conservationists, and cattle ranchers have saved the buffalo from extinction.

Check In Why was the buffalo important to Native Americans?

Discuss

1. What connections can you make among the four selections in this book? How do you think the selections are related?

2. How does the folk tale of Long Arrow show the importance of the horse to the Blackfoot people?

3. Why do you think Chief Crazy Horse is still remembered by Americans today?

4. Do you think Buffalo Bill was more of a friend or more of an enemy to the buffalo? Why? Support your opinion.

5. What do you still wonder about the Native Americans of the Great Plains and the issues and events that have been important in their history?